LET'S EXPLORE THE SOLAR SYSTEM
(Planets)

Speedy Publishing LLC
40 E. Main St. #1156
Newark, DE 19711
www.speedypublishing.com

The Solar System refers to a star and all the objects that orbit it, either directly or indirectly.

Our solar system comprises the sun, eight planets and their natural satellites, dwarf planets, asteroids and comets. The eight planets are Mercury, Venus, Earth, Mars, Jupiter, Saturn, Uranus, Neptune.

The Sun is the star at the center of the Solar System. The sun is the primary source of energy for life on Earth.

Mercury is the smallest and closest planet to the Sun. Mercury has the thinnest atmosphere of any planet in the solar system. Mercury has no moons or rings because of its low gravity and lack of atmosphere.

Venus is the second planet from the Sun. Venus is the hottest planet in our solar system, the average surface temperature is 462 °C.

Earth is the third planet from the Sun. It is the densest planet in the Solar System. 70% of the Earth's surface is covered by water.

Mars is the fourth planet from the Sun. It is the second smallest planet in the Solar System. Mars is often described as the "Red Planet" due to its reddish appearance.

Jupiter is the fifth planet from the Sun. It is the largest planet in the Solar System. Jupiter is the fourth brightest object in the solar system. Jupiter's interior is made of rock, metal, and hydrogen compounds.

Saturn is the sixth planet from the Sun. It is the second largest planet in the Solar System. Saturn has 150 moons and smaller moonlets. Saturn is a gas giant made up mostly of hydrogen and helium.

Uranus is the seventh planet from the Sun. Uranus is the coldest planet in the solar system. It is often referred to as the "ice giant".

Neptune is the eighth and farthest planet from the Sun. Neptune has a very thin collection of rings. Neptune has 14 known moons.

The Moon is Earth's only natural satellite. The moon is the easiest celestial object to find in the night sky. The Moon is the fifth largest natural satellite in the Solar System.

A dwarf planet is a planetary-mass object that is neither a planet nor a natural satellite. There are 5 officially recognized dwarf planets in our solar system, they are Ceres, Pluto, Haumea, Makemake and Eris. Pluto is the largest dwarf planet.

The asteroid belt is the region of the Solar System located roughly between the orbits of the planets Mars and Jupiter.
The asteroid belt contains hundreds of thousands of known asteroids

www.ingramcontent.com/pod-product-compliance
Lightning Source LLC
Chambersburg PA
CBHW080611170726
48004CB00019B/1800
9798869453242